FIND THE WORDS

AN A-TO-Z GUIDE TO HELP YOU
WRITE CONTENT WITH
CONFIDENCE

Nandini Chatto

Copyright © 2023 by Nandini Chatto.

All rights reserved. No part of this publication may be reproduced, distributed or transmitted in any form or by any means, including photocopying, recording, or other electronic or mechanical methods, without the prior written permission of the publisher, except in the case of brief quotations embodied in critical reviews and certain other non-commercial uses permitted by copyright law.

Find The Words: An A-to-Z guide to help you write content with confidence / Nandini Chatto —1st edition

ISBN: 978-1-3999-5037-4

CONTENTS

INTRODUCTION 5

AUDIENCE 8
BE DIRECT 9
CASE STUDIES 11
DIGITAL CONTENT 13
EDITING 15
FEATURES VS BENEFITS 16
GRAMMAR 18
HOUSE STYLE 19
IMAGINE YOUR READER
 IN FRONT OF YOU 20
JARGON-FREE ZONE 21
KNOW, FEEL, DO............................ 23
LAYOUT 24
MESSAGE 25
NEVER USE A LONG WORD
 WHEN A SHORT ONE WILL DO 26
ONE IDEA PER SENTENCE................. 27
PURPOSE 28
QUALITY NOT QUANTITY 29
READ IT OUT ALOUD 30
SUBHEADINGS 31
TONE OF VOICE 32
UPDATE WEBSITE CONTENT
 REGULARLY 33
VARY THE LENGTH OF
 YOUR SENTENCES 34

CONTENTS — CONTINUED

WOULD I WANT TO READ THIS? 36
XMAS AND OTHER ABBREVIATIONS 37
YOU CAN BREAK SCHOOL RULES 38
ZZZ 39

Introduction

This book will help you to transform the way you write content at work.

Most of us write content as part of our job these days – things like web pages, reports, articles, posts, emails and so on.

Good content really matters, because it helps you to tell your stories and reach a wider audience.

But many people have never had any guidance about how to approach it. So they aren't sure where to start and feel stuck.

The good news is that writing content doesn't have to be complicated. That's why I wrote this book.

Find The Words will help you to plan your content, write clearly, and connect with your audience.

How to use this book

Wherever you are in your content journey, this book will meet you there.

Got too many ideas and can't get started? Go to 'Know, Feel, Do' and 'Message' to get your thoughts in order.

Perhaps you've already written something, but it doesn't sound right? Check out 'Editing' and 'Would I want to read this?'.

Or maybe you need clarity on who you're writing for. In that case 'Audience' is your first port of call.

You can also read the whole book and use the guidance to gradually take your content to the next level.

Just keep it on your desk and refer to it whenever you write anything.

About me
I'm a content writer and journalist who's been working with words for over 15 years.

Based in the UK, I've written marketing materials, journalism pieces, video scripts, websites and case studies for a range of organisations.

I know that some people feel confused about content writing. In fact, my colleagues used to come to me for guidance about it all the time.

So I designed and ran workshops to help them write content with confidence.

Now I want to do the same for you. That's why I've taken my 26 best bits of guidance and turned them into a book.

And now it's over to you. Apply the tips, get creative with the exercises, and enjoy the content writing process.

Let's get writing.

Audience

Before you write a single word, you need to know who you're writing for.

This is crucial because the tone, language and messaging will change depending on your audience.

Think of it as the difference between an email you would write for your manager, and one you'd send to a friend.

Start by asking yourself these questions about your audience:
- What's their profession, age range, location and so on?
- What are their interests and problems?
- How does my product/service/offering relate to their life?

As you do this, create a real person in your mind.

This will enable you to write content that *speaks directly to your audience*.

Be Direct

To ensure readability, make sure your content gets to the point. Here are two tips to make your writing more direct.

TIP ONE

Put your key messages at the start – don't bury them in the middle. If your readers can't find what they need quickly and easily, you'll lose them.

For example:

BEFORE
On Monday 20 April in the afternoon, following the awards ceremony and lunch, the CEO's office will be the venue for the Strategy Board meeting at 3pm.

AFTER
The Strategy Board will meet on Monday 20 April at 3pm in the CEO's office, following the awards ceremony and lunch.

TIP TWO: Be Direct

Use 'We', 'You', 'Your' and 'Us'. This will make your writing sound direct, personal and transparent.

For example:

BEFORE
Customers are requested to send their feedback via email. The team will go through these to see how the product can be improved.

AFTER
We want to know what you think. Send us your feedback by email, and we will use your insights to improve the product.

Case Studies

Case studies are a great source of content because they show the world how you've solved someone's problem or made their life easier.

How do you find case studies?

Speak to the people who've benefitted from your work. Talk to your satisfied customers.

Use their stories to create content that will help you to build trust, promote your work and reach more people.

Case study content can be adapted and used across your communications. For example on your website, marketing materials, company reports, social media posts – the list goes on.

So it's worth taking the time to find them and use them.

Need some inspiration? Try the exercise on the next page.

EXERCISE: Case Studies

Find two or three satisfied customers, and ask them these questions:
- What do you like about our product/service/offering?
- How has it improved your life?
- Why would you recommend it to others?

Now get creative about how you're going to use the content from these case studies.

Digital Content

Digital content isn't like printed content – people read it in a different way.

They scan and skim, quickly trying to find what they need. So the way you write online needs to reflect this.

When it comes to websites, research shows that well-structured pages designed for scanning are the ones that are most likely to get read.

Here are some tips and an exercise to help you achieve this.

TIPS for writing website content:

- Keep sentences at 10–12 words, and paragraphs at 2–3 sentences.
- Include bullet points and subheadings.
- Highlight important phrases in bold.
- Add your 'call to action' early on, and again at the end.

EXERCISE: Digital Content

- Look at the three most viewed pages on your website.
- Are they easy to skim read?
- How can you use these tips to improve them?

Editing

Editing ensures that your content is clear and easy to understand.

You can do this in two stages. In the first edit, read what you've written and ask yourself:
- Will the structure and messaging make sense to my audience?
- Is there a clear call to action?

This is the time to add/delete things, and to restructure your content.

In the second edit, cut out unnecessary words and sharpen your sentences.

TIP

Proofread your final draft. Proofreading (which isn't the same as editing) is the final check for those tiny spelling mistakes or missing words.

However, mistakes sometimes still happen and that's ok – we're all human after all!

Features vs Benefits

When you write persuasive content, start with the benefits of your product/service/offering to grab people's attention.

Your readers are thinking: "What's in it for me?" so instead of just listing the features, highlight the benefits first.

The questions to think about are:
- What are you 'selling'?
- Who to?
- How will it impact their life?

Not sure where to start with benefits? Does your product or service:
- improve lives
- save time or money
- increase knowledge/add insight?

Once you've identified the benefits, you have a starting point for creating persuasive content.

EXERCISE: Features vs Benefits

- Select a product or service that you offer.
- Write down the ways it benefits the end user.
- Now get creative. How can you use this information to write content that'll grab people's attention?

Grammar

Good grammar makes your content sound credible and trustworthy.

But grammar is a complex subject that many people struggle with.

The good news is that sorting out grammar issues doesn't have to be time-consuming.

It's easy to check specific grammar questions online, eg just type "What's the difference between your and you're" into a search engine to find the answer.

I also use online dictionaries which usually have helpful sections about grammar.

House Style

Many organisations have a 'house style' – a set of rules for their written content.

It typically includes things like:
- how to write dates and times
- when to use capital letters
- styles for fonts and bullet points.

House styles ensure that there is consistency across all content. They are also part of your overall corporate brand.

So don't let yours sit on a shelf and gather dust!

Make sure you apply it to every piece of writing that you produce.

Imagine your reader in front of you

Many workplaces still use corporate language in their content.

So they end up sounding like a robot rather than a human being.

But to really change the way you connect with your audience, you need to write with an authentic, human voice.

What's the best way to do this?

Imagine that your reader is in front of you, and you're having a conversation with them. Write down *what* you'd say, and *how* you'd say it.

This will make you sound like a real person, and your readers will think that you're speaking directly to them.

Jargon-Free Zone

Sometimes at work people say things like: "Let's think outside the box" and "We can touch base this afternoon".

This is known as business jargon. And this kind of language can creep into an organisation's content as well.

But jargon will confuse your readers.

Also known as cliches, buzzwords and management-speak, jargon can often be reduced to just one or two words.

Sometimes you can take it out completely without changing the meaning of a sentence.

Here are some examples of jargon and what to use instead:

BEFORE
I don't agree with the new policy **in any way, shape or form**. **At the end of the day**, the responsibility for this lies with the CEO.

AFTER
I don't agree with the new policy. **Ultimately**, the responsibility for this lies with the CEO.

BEFORE
These databases are no longer **fit for purpose**. **Going forward**, I'd like to see some changes.

AFTER
These databases don't **meet the right standards** anymore. **In future**, I'd like to see some changes.

BEFORE
We will launch this new initiative with a series of **deliverables**.

AFTER
We will launch this new initiative with **user guides and a helpline**.

EXERCISE: Jargon-Free Zone

- Write down three examples of workplace jargon that annoy you. Get colleagues involved in this as well.
- What do these phrases mean in plain English?
- Can you improve your content – and the way you connect with your audience – by using the plain English version of these phrases?

Know, Feel, Do

Use this framework whenever you write a piece of content. Before you start writing, ask yourself:

What do I want my readers to KNOW?
-What are my important messages?

How do I want my readers to FEEL?
-Informed, excited, angry, inspired etc?
-Am I appealing to their head, heart, or both?

What do I want my readers to DO?
-Read a report, buy a product/service, listen to a podcast etc?

This framework can be applied to any type of content – emails, web pages, marketing campaigns and more.

Layout
How will your words appear on the page?

Layout isn't just about design, it's about content as well.

Good layout presents information in a logical way, makes the important bits stand out and is easy to navigate. This applies to both printed and online content.

TIPS for good layout:

- Make sure there's enough white space: give your writing room to breathe.
- Break up large chunks of text.
- Use bullet points and subheadings to signpost readers.
- Think about how your readers will see the content laid out – eg a double-page spread in a magazine, or on a smartphone. Adapt your content based on that.

Message

What's your message? Be clear about this BEFORE you start writing.

Ask yourself:
- What are my key messages?
- Why is this interesting for my readers?
- What action do I want readers to take?

This step comes after 'Audience' to give you a content framework that you can use every time:

- Audience
- Message
- Action

Never use a long word when a short one will do

This is one of George Orwell's six rules for writing, which he set out in his 1946 essay: *Politics and the English Language*.

This rule is also relevant to modern-day content writing.

For example:

BEFORE
I would like to **utilise** your training materials. Are they available to **purchase**?

AFTER
I would like to **use** your training materials. Are they available to **buy**?

Shorter words keep your content uncluttered, and your readers won't have to wade through long words to get to the key points.

One idea per sentence

Long sentences crammed with lots of ideas can work in creative writing, but not in business content.

Your readers will find it hard to follow and they'll lose the message.

To ensure clarity – and make life easy for your readers – take the 'one idea per sentence' approach.

TIP

Here's a guide to the ideal sentence length:

- for print it's 15–20 words
- for digital it's 10–12 words.

Purpose

What's the purpose of your content? How will it serve your audience?

Use this framework to help you get clarity:

This [*insert content type*] is designed to [*insert purpose*] for [*insert audience*].

After they've read the content, I want my audience to [*insert action*].

Quality not Quantity

Are you signed-up to a mailing list that sends you endless newsletters you never read? How do you feel when you get that type of content?

If you don't want your audience to feel like that, then 'quality not quantity' needs to be part of your overall content strategy.

It's not about producing endless content just for the sake of it. Ask yourself:
- How can I use content to serve my audience?
- Can I produce less content, but give more value?
- What do I want to achieve with my content over the next 12 months?

See 'Purpose' as well to help you with this.

Read it out aloud
Once you've written your content, read it out aloud.

Did you stumble anywhere?

If you did, that's where you need to rewrite it.

Subheadings

Subheadings act as signposts for your readers.

They break up the text, give readers an overview of what you're saying, and enable them to find the bits that they're interested in.

Subheadings can be used in different types of content, such as articles and website pages.

TIP

Make your subheadings clear and specific.

For example on an About Us web page, use '30 years' experience' rather than 'Our story'.

Tone of Voice

Tone of Voice is how your organisation's personality comes through in its writing.

For example, that personality could be: serious, professional, quirky, humorous and so on.

Your Tone of Voice represents your brand values, and is an opportunity to connect with people.

So it needs to be reflected in everything you write to ensure consistency.

Tone of Voice is also linked to 'House Style'. Always make sure that the two things work together.

Update website content regularly

There may be some content on your website that needs to be updated regularly.

For example, do you have a web page for an event that has already taken place? Update the page after the event, and add a link to next year's event page.

Check your site for links that are broken, or that take you to the wrong place, and replace them.

This will ensure that your website content is always fresh and up-to-date.

TIPS

- Make this part of your overall content strategy.
- Add a note in your calendar to update website content every six or 12 months.

Vary the length of your sentences
This is a quick way to spice up your writing.

When every sentence is the same length, the content can feel a bit dull.

Long sentences are hard to read. And your readers will notice if they all start the same way.

The solution? Vary the length and structure of your sentences.

This changes the pace and rhythm, and gives the reader variety. Here's a non-business example:

BEFORE
She felt embarrassed as she walked into the team meeting half-an-hour late again. She whispered an apology to everyone.

AFTER
She felt embarrassed as she walked into the team meeting half-an-hour late. Again.
'Sorry everyone,' she whispered.

TIP

Vary the length and structure by:

- breaking up long sentences
- changing the way you start sentences
- using different lengths.

Would I want to read this?
This approach can make a big difference to the quality of your content.

When you've finished writing, ask yourself:
- Does this keep me interested?
- Does it give me the information I need?
- Is everything here necessary?
- Will my readers care about it?

If the answer to any of these is 'no', make some tweaks and turn it into something you'd want to read yourself.

Xmas, and other abbreviations

Use abbreviations and acronyms sparingly.

Your readers won't necessarily know what you're referring to.

Someone reading your website in another country might not know the cultural references that are obvious to you.

To ensure clarity, write out the abbreviation/acronym in full the first time, with the letters in brackets. After that, just use the letters.

For example:
National Health Service (NHS), Christmas (Xmas).

You can break school rules
I'm talking about the rules we learned at school about how to write sentences.

Those rules are fine for essays, but writing at work is a different matter.

Sometimes those rules stay with you, and it feels strange to write in any other way. But you can break them!

While good grammar and spelling are still important, you can finish a sentence with a preposition if you want to.

And you can start a sentence with 'and' or 'but' if it feels right.

The key here is to focus on the needs of your audience and use your Tone of Voice.

Zzz...
Dull content makes readers want to go to sleep. So make sure you leave your readers excited, inspired, and wide awake.

TIP

Two quick ways to make dull writing more interesting are covered in B and V.

Step one: Be direct.

Step two: Vary the length and structure of your sentences.

These steps will add some spice to your writing, and keep your readers interested.

YOUR NOTES

www.ingramcontent.com/pod-product-compliance
Lightning Source LLC
Chambersburg PA
CBHW030459010526
44118CB00011B/1014